# Tunes for Cornet Technic

## by
### Fred Weber
### and
### Major Herman Vincent

## To The Teacher

One of the most effective and enjoyable ways to develop technical dexterity on an instrument is through melodies of a technical nature with scale and rhythm variation based on familiar melodies. TUNES FOR TECHNIC is designed with this in mind. Because tunes, melodies and technical variations are interesting and more enjoyable to practice, most students will work more effectively, and over-all results will be excellent. Some of the melodies and variations in TUNES FOR TECHNIC may be challenging and difficult. In this case work up slowly and accurately, then gradually increase tempo. In general, the book progresses in difficulty and correlates with the method book, "The Cornet Student," Part I, and may be also used in conjunction with any elementary cornet method.

The Belwin "STUDENT INSTRUMENTAL COURSE" - A course for individual and class instruction of LIKE instruments, at three levels, for all band instruments.

*EACH BOOK IS COMPLETE IN ITSELF BUT ALL BOOKS ARE CORRELATED WITH EACH OTHER*

### METHOD
### "The Cornet Student"
#### For individual
#### or
#### brass class instruction.

*ALTHOUGH EACH BOOK CAN BE USED SEPARATELY, IDEALLY, ALL SUPPLEMENTARY BOOKS SHOULD BE USED AS COMPANION BOOKS WITH THE METHOD*

### STUDIES AND MELODIOUS ETUDES

Supplementary scales, warm-up and technical drills, musicianship studies and melody-like studies.

### TUNES FOR TECHNIC

Technical type melodies, variations, and "famous passages" from musical literature --- for the development of technical dexterity.

### THE CORNET SOLOIST

Interesting and playable graded easy solo arrangements of famous and well-liked melodies. Also contains 2 Duets, and 1 Trio. Easy piano accompaniments.

### DUETS FOR STUDENTS

Easy duet arrangements of familiar melodies for early ensemble experience.
Available for: Flute
            B♭ Clarinet
            Alto Sax
            B♭ Cornet
            Trombone

# CONTENTS

# Old MacDonald

# Pop Goes The Weazel

# Yankee Doodle

# Looby Lou

4

# Sweet Rosie O'Grady

Nugent

# Down In The Valley

# Tramp-Tramp-Tramp

Geo. Root

# Poet and Peasant
*Waltz*

# Sidewalks Of New York

# American Hymn

B.I.C.148

6

## The Band Played On

Ward

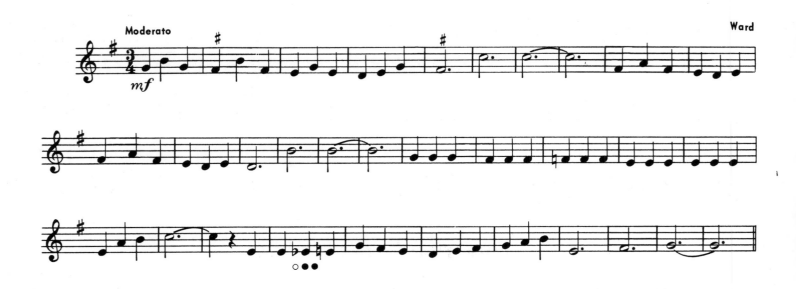

## Annie Rooney

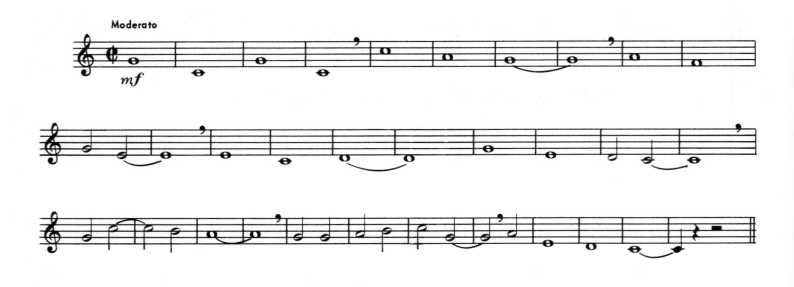

## Minnie Tee-Hee
### *The Indian Maid*

Weber

There was once an In - dian Dame, Min - nie Tee - Hee was her name,

Her big sis - ter had more fame, She was Min - nie Ha! Ha!

# The Victors

Ebel

# Hungarian Dance Theme

Brahms

# Theme From High School Cadets March

Sousa

# Swanee River

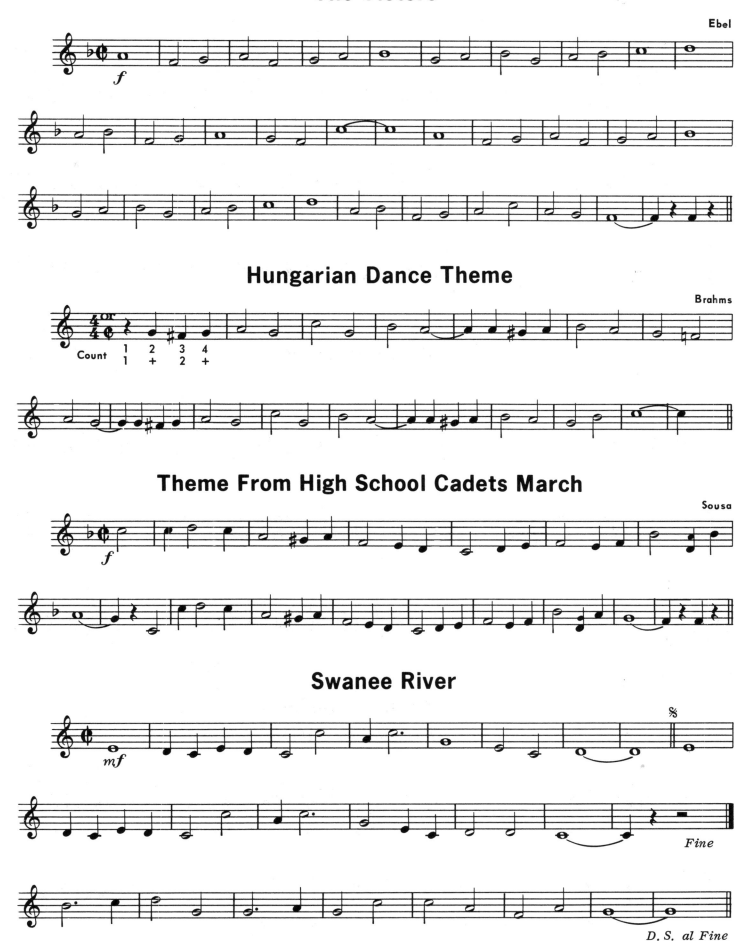

*Fine*

*D. S. al Fine*

B.I.C.148

# Onward Christian Soldiers March

A. Sullivan

# El Capitan Theme

Sousa

# Rifle Regiment

Sousa

# Home Sweet Home

Bishop

# Joyce's 71st Regiment

Boyer

# Entry Of The Gladiator March

Fucik

# Theme From High School Cadets March

Sousa

# Sleeping Beauty Waltz

# S. I. B. A. March

# Rainbow Theme

## Sakura Sakura
### *A Japanese Folk Tune*

## Fiesta

## Russian Melody

# Long Long Ago

# Long Long Ago

## Birthday Greetings

# Buffalo Gals

# Up On The House-Top

# Wearing Of The Green

# The Erie Canal

# Comin' Round The Mountain

# VARIATIONS ON A FAMOUS THEME

Work this page out Carefully, then try for Speed

Mozart

### Melody

### Rhythm Variation I in Key of F

### Rhythm Variation II in Key of C

### Scale Variation I in Key of F

### Scale Variation II in Key of C

B.I.C.148

# The Blue Bells Of Scotland

# Loch Lomond

# Our Director

Bigelow

# Melody In F

Rubinstein

B.I.C.148

# THEME AND VARIATIONS

# The Dying Cowboy

# Cara Nome

# Sharpshooters March

# TUNES AND VARIATIONS
## Polly Wolly Doodle

### Marine's March

B.I.C.148

# Can Can

# Under The Double Eagle

# Father Of Victory

# Auld Lang Syne

# Hymn Of Thanksgiving

# Adeste Fidelis

# VARIATION
## America The Beautiful

*Tonguing Fun*

Moderato

Ward

## Jewish Folk Song

## The Violins Play

Paganini

*Fine*

*D.S. al Fine*

# In The Gloaming

# Our Boys Will Shine Tonight

# Ta-Ra-Ra-Boom-te-ay

# Blow The Man Down

## Tonguing Variation

# Santa Lucia

# Gypsy Rondo

*Work out Carefully then try for Speed.*

## A Technical Tune

Haydn

*Fine*

*D. C. al Fine*

# Melody In Key Of D

## A Tonguing Tune

# Massa's In De Cold, Cold Ground

Duvernoy

*ritard*

# Eyes Of Texas

# Melody By Borodin

Borodin

# Tschaikowsky Concerto Theme

Tschaikowsky

B.I.C.148

## Hinky Dinky Parley - Voo

## Merry Widow

Lehar

## Song Of The Reaper

R. Schuman

## Drink To Me Only

## Gold And Silver Waltz

Lehar

## Greensleeves

B.I.C.148

# Carnival Of Venice With Variations

**Slowly**

**March tempo**

*Scale Variation*

*Work out carefully, then try for speed.*

## Theme From The Thunderer March

Sousa

## Dance

Streabog

*Fine*

*D. C. al Fine*

## Mail Call

## Dance

Purcell

## Mess Call

Use 1st and 3rd valves throughout.

B.I.C.148

*Work out all Melodies on this page Carefully, then try for Speed with Accuracy*

## Trepak

Tschaikowsky

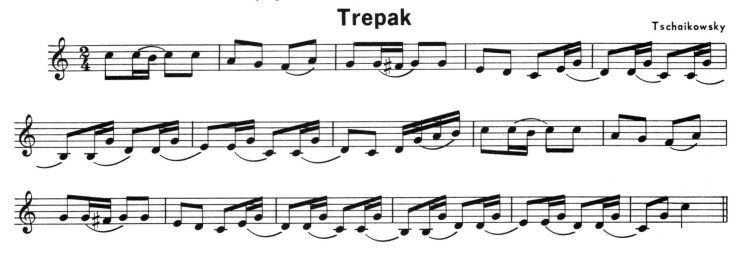

## Variation On Yankee Doodle

## Moment Musical

Schubert

B.I.C.148

*Work out all Melodies on this Page carefully, then try for speed with accuracy*

## Reuben Reuben

*Technical Variation*

## Jingle Bells

*Scale Variation*

*Work out all Melodies on this Page carefully, then try for speed with accuracy.*

## Morris Dance

Edw. German

Fine

D. C. al Fine

## Melody From The Opera Carmen

Bizet

## Arkansas Traveler

Folk Tune